Talking Lawrence

Patterns of Eastwood dialect in the work of D. H. Lawrence

Hilary Hillier

Critical, Cultural and Communications Press
in association with the D. H. Lawrence Research Centre,
University of Nottingham

Nottingham

2008

Nottingham Lawrence Studies
General editors: Sean Matthews and Macdonald Daly

Talking Lawrence: Patterns of Eastwood dialect in the work of D. H. Lawrence,
by Hilary Hillier.

First published in Great Britain by Critical, Cultural and Communications Press in association with the D. H. Lawrence Research Centre, University of Nottingham, 2008.

Cover design by Hannibal.

Contents

About the author

Hilary Hillier is a Fellow of the D. H. Lawrence Research Centre at the University of Nottingham. She has taught and lectured to undergraduate and postgraduate students on a range of English language subjects, particularly English social and regional accents and dialects, and on D. H. Lawrence. Her principal research interest is the grammar of the dialect of Eastwood and the Erewash Valley. She co-directed the 'Odour of Chrysanthemums' digitization project in the Centre's collaboration with Manuscripts and Special Collections and the Higher Education Academy's English Subject Centre. Her publications include *Analysing Real Texts: Research Studies in Modern English Language*, published by Palgrave Macmillan in 2004, and 'Community, family, 'Morel': a dialect approach to *Sons and Lovers*', to appear in the proceedings of the 11th D. H. Lawrence International Conference, *2007: Return to Eastwood*, forthcoming from CCC Press. She was born and brought up in Eastwood, the daughter and granddaughter of miners. In bringing together her work on the dialect of Eastwood and on Lawrence, this book represents a unique conjunction of significant professional and personal concerns.

About Nottingham Lawrence Studies

The D. H. Lawrence Research Centre at the University of Nottingham was founded in 1990 to provide a focus for research and teaching in Lawrence Studies, and to promote the Lawrence Collections. The Centre hosts conferences, symposia and lectures, as well as coordinating Lawrence-related classes and courses at undergraduate and postgraduate level. We also work closely with Lawrence Societies around the world, particularly the Eastwood D. H. Lawrence Society, and offer support for Visiting Scholars wishing to use the Lawrence Collections.

Nottingham Lawrence Studies was established in 2008 to publish work in the field. We welcome submissions, and proposals, of work of interest to academics, students and general readers. These should be sent to:

The D. H. Lawrence Research Centre
School of English Studies
University of Nottingham
University Park
Nottingham
United Kingdom
NG7 2RD
Email: **Sean.Matthews@nottingham.ac.uk**

Preface

There have been several books published in the course of the last few years that are devoted to the study of dialects, that is, to the ways in which language varies according to different speakers, different parts of the country and different social and cultural contexts. But there have been few that look specifically at how dialects can be described for the purposes of better understanding the uses of language in the work of major writers. Hilary Hillier's *Talking Lawrence* is an innovative and detailed introduction to some key patterns in the use of the regional dialect and accent of Eastwood in the early writings of D. H. Lawrence. Writing from her own direct experience as a native of the region and from many years experience as a sociolinguist, Hilary Hillier offers a framework for students and readers of Lawrence to enhance their understanding of such uses of language. It is a framework which focuses not simply on vocabulary and pronunciation, as is the case with many dialect studies, but on the grammar of the dialect too.

Standard English is the norm against which other dialects are measured and in this book Hilary Hillier shows the ways in which the grammar, vocabulary and pronunciation of the Eastwood dialect varies from standard language norms. A dialect is often understood as an inferior form of language and as somehow a series of mistakes relative to standard forms of the language. As a sociolinguist Hilary Hiller shows that standard English is a dialect too. It is a prestige dialect used for a range of social purposes and like all dialects encodes the social class, identities and affiliations of those who choose to speak it or not to speak it in particular social contexts. D. H. Lawrence is highly sensitive to the social and social class implications of (and attitudes towards) such choices and carefully weaves such understanding into the way he represents the speech of his characters. The exemplary descriptions provided by Hilary Hillier enable us to identify the subtle ways in which social positions and personal relationships are encoded and negotiated between the characters in many of Lawrence's most important early stories, novels and plays. The book will be of particular interest to speakers of other languages interested in Lawrence studies but it also provides an authoritative platform for anyone concerned to explore more fully and systematically the key meanings which always emerge when language and its use for literary purposes is at stake.

Ronald Carter
Professor of Modern English Language
School of English Studies
University of Nottingham

1 Lawrence and the dialect

D. H. Lawrence makes extensive and significant use of the authentic dialect of Eastwood and the Erewash Valley in a number of his stories, novels and plays. The dialect, in fact, serves to define the working class mining community in which he grew up and in which these works are set; it constitutes one of the ways in which he continued to reassert his roots in that community. A basic grasp of the patterning of the different elements of the dialect can deepen our appreciation of the ways in which Lawrence chooses to use the language he knew so well.

I am a linguist, interested in the way that language varies according to the social background and particular circumstances of the people using it. Some years ago I wanted to collect material for teaching undergraduate and postgraduate students about regional variation in English accents and dialects, and, since I was born and brought up in Eastwood, it was natural that I should turn my attention to the dialect spoken in my home territory.

In 1991 I began work on a small research project designed to record and transcribe the conversational speech of small groups of children in two Eastwood primary schools. The chosen schools were Devonshire Drive Infants and Junior, which had been my own primary school, and Greasley Beauvale Infants, which had been D. H. Lawrence's school. Many hours of talk were recorded, of which only a fraction has yet been transcribed, and an even smaller fraction subjected to detailed analysis.

Lawrence had in fact been built into the project more or less from the outset: how far – if at all – might the dialect used in his work still be found in Eastwood today? The Lawrence element proved, however, to have great practical value too. Transcribing natural speech is not an easy task, and the more informal the talk the less easy its transcription becomes. Dialect speech compounds the difficulty. The fact that Lawrence has to some extent 'fixed' the dialect for us by writing it down means that his texts can perform an invaluable 'checking' function: direct comparisons can be made between instances of naturally-occurring Eastwood speech and Lawrence's representations of similar constructions given to his characters. This can be especially useful for vestigial or 'omitted' features or sounds. The 'real' language can be compared with its 'literary' representation, and vice versa, to the benefit of both.

My own main interest is in identifying and describing the grammatical patterns of the dialect, together with its corresponding pronunciation patterns. This book, therefore, sets out a basic framework for describing the patterns which seem to be the most clearly identifiable. The work is still ongoing, and the framework has to be adjusted and expanded as more spoken data and more Lawrence texts are subjected to detailed analysis. This little book, therefore, should be regarded as 'the story so far…' However, to answer one of the initial questions of the project: the dialect would seem to be alive and well in Eastwood and the Erewash Valley. Many of the dialect forms found in Lawrence's work – and illustrated in this book – can indeed still be heard in the area. 'Real' examples of these are presented in Chapter 4.

Lawrence's use of dialect is usually thought of in terms of his choice of individual words – that is, his use of a particular regional vocabulary, some of it now archaic. Many editions of his works in fact provide extensive glossaries which cover vocabulary, particularly useful ones being found in Baron and Baron's 1994 edition of *Sons and Lovers*, and Schwarze and Worthen's 1999 edition of *The Plays*. (The glossary of words and phrases in Appendix 2 is indebted in part to those editions.)

It is important to recognise, however, that any dialect of British English, whether standard or non-standard, should also be regarded as a particular collection of linguistic features of structure (its characteristic grammar) and pronunciation (its characteristic accent). These features form recognisable patterns, and particular combinations of features are likely to vary in identifiable and systematic ways according to the regional and social background of any group of speakers in any given context. There is a correlation between the social class of speakers (roughly defined by level of education, income, type of occupation, etc.) and the degree to which regional features of pronunciation and, especially, grammar occur in their speech.

In broad terms, therefore, non-standard grammatical features will tend to correlate with a 'strong' (or 'broad') regional accent (that is, one having many regional pronunciation features) and also with 'working class'. Spoken standard English grammar, usually with a number of regional pronunciation features, will tend to correlate with 'middle class'. The non-regional 'Received Pronunciation' (RP) – often informally called 'BBC English' – is spoken by only a tiny proportion of the population of the British Isles. It is, however, the accent which is accorded the highest prestige. (Much more extended and detailed introductions to the factors influencing speech variation in English can be found in Part I of Milroy and Milroy, eds, 1993, and Chapter 1 of Hughes, Trudgill and Watt, 2005.)

It is consistent with this broad linguistic theory that Lawrence should show the characters who represent his fictional working class mining communities using many features of both non-standard grammar and regional pronunciation. This book is intended to set out a framework for identifying and categorising individual dialect features which readers can then use as an analytical tool – as a means of 'measuring' the careful social distinctions Lawrence makes between his different characters. We can see how some characters use many, and many different, non-standard features while others use fewer and some perhaps none at all. We can also explore how far, and in what way, individual characters may be shown to modify their use of certain features according to subtle shifts of situation and mood. (The use of the second person singular pronoun *thou* can be particularly revealing in this respect.)

The following pages, therefore, present a framework for describing some of the patterns of grammar and pronunciation in the dialect speech of Eastwood and the Erewash Valley. Individual grammatical features are grouped under main headings identifying selected parts of speech; these headings are presented in alphabetical order for reference purposes only, with no order of priority or importance implied. Comparisons are made with standard British English grammar in each case. Pronunciation features are compared with those of 'Received Pronunciation' (RP). A glossary of the main grammatical and other terms used in the frameworks is given in Appendix 1. The glossary is, of course, a much-simplified and inevitably superficial set of definitions of the terms used: readers are urged to flesh out this account by consulting some of the sources given in the annotated bibliography in Appendix 3.

Illustrative examples from Lawrence's works are cited under each heading of the grammatical framework in Chapter 2. The relevant non-standard feature in the particular example is highlighted in ***bold italics*;** omissions are indicated via ***[ ]***. Sometimes both standard and non-standard forms may be used in the same extracted example (for example, Mrs Hemstock's ***th' door*** and *the bucket* under III (a). Only non-standard forms are highlighted. Sometimes more than one kind of non-standard form may be used in an individual example, that is, in addition to the particular form highlighted. Only the non-standard form currently under discussion will be highlighted. The additional form may be shown, and highlighted, under a different heading: for example, in Father's ...*you' wiser than them as knows, you are*, relative pronoun ***as*** is highlighted under VII (e) and his omission of *'re* in *you **[']** wiser* under VIII (e).

The examples are taken from six selected works by Lawrence. The extracts are very short and inevitably have to be read out of context. Nevertheless many of them give vivid – indeed sparkling – snapshots of the various characters portrayed: for example, Mrs Hemstock, Mrs Smalley, Mrs Gascoyne and Mrs Purdy. They also provide convincing evidence of Lawrence's ability to convey emotional power and (especially) humour through dialogue alone. (They may even succeed in persuading readers to explore some less familiar texts.)

Titles and editions of the chosen works are listed below. Titles of works are cited for each example in abbreviated form as shown, e.g. ***OC***, ***SL***, ***CFN*** etc., together with page and line numbers in the following form 197: 27. These relate to the specific edition mentioned, but Part or Chapter numbers or Act and Scene numbers are also given to enable readers to refer to editions other than the ones listed here:

'Odour of Chrysanthemums' (in *The Prussian Officer and other Stories*, ed. John Worthen, Cambridge: Cambridge University Press, 1983; London: Penguin, 1995) (***OC***)

Sons and Lovers (ed. Helen Baron and Carl Baron, Cambridge: Cambridge University Press, 1992; London: Penguin, 1994) (***SL***)

A Collier's Friday Night (in *The Plays*, ed. Hans-Wilhelm Schwarze and John Worthen, Cambridge: Cambridge University Press, 1999) ***(CFN)***

The Widowing of Mrs Holroyd (in *The Plays*, as above) (***WH***)

The Merry-go-Round (in *The Plays*, as above) (***MGR***)

The Daughter- in-Law (in *The Plays*, as above) (***DL***)

2 Grammatical patterns (compared with Standard British English grammar)

I Adverbs

I (a) without *–ly*:

He went ***peaceful***, Lizzie – peaceful as sleep. (***OC***, Part II, 197: 27, Grandmother)

There isn't a more ***truthful*** spoken lad in the Bottoms. (***SL***, Chapter III, 65: 34-5, Mrs Anthony)

…I'm sure you get on wonderfully – wonderfully – considering….Yes – ah'n non done so ***bad***, I think. (***CFN***, Act II, 23: 21-3, Mother and Barker)

Some women could have lived with him ***happy*** enough. An' a fat lot you'd have thanked me for my telling. (***WH***, Act III, 99: 24-5, Grandmother)

My mother worna one ter handle you very ***tender***: 'er wor rough, not like thee. (***MGR***, Act II, Scene 3, 148: 30-1, Harry)

She'll settle down ***comfortable***, lad. (***DL***, Act I, Scene 2, 329: 32, Mrs Purdy)

I (b) ***fair*** as intensifier (equivalent of *really*, *quite*):

It [the fire]'s so red, and full of little caves – and it feels so nice, and you can ***fair*** smell it. (***OC***, Part I, 185: 19-20, Annie)

…that doesn't give him [William] a right to get hold of the boy's collar, an' ***fair*** rip it clean off his back. (***SL***, Chapter III, 66: 15-16, Mrs Anthony)

I know the things I bring down from ours, they ***fair*** damp in a day. (***CFN***, Act I, 11: 27, Gertie Coomber)

She ***fair*** pines for our Harry, yet she'd have Job Arthur for fear of getting nobody. (***MGR***, Act IV, 170: 28-9, Mrs Smalley)

Eh, how 'er did but scraight an' cry. It ***fair*** turned me ower. (***DL***, Act I, Scene 2, 328: 21, Mrs Purdy)

I (c) ***that*** as intensifier (equivalent of *so*):

A man gets ***that*** caked up wi' th' dust, you know, ***that*** clogged up, down a coal mine, he *needs* a drink when he comes home. (***SL***, Chapter II, 47: 8-9, Morel)

Then [Taffy] he slives up an' shoves 'is 'ead on yer, ***that*** cadin'. (***SL***, Chapter IV, 89: 23-4, Morel)

We mustn't let him set, he'll be ***that*** heavy, bless him. (***WH***, Act III, 106: 39-40, Grandmother)

It is [the case] wi' a woman who's ***that*** cunning at kissin' an' cuddlin' that a man's fair smockravelled… (***MGR***, Act I, Scene 1, 120: 16-17, Mrs Hemstock)

Er wor ***that*** high an' mighty, 'er wanted summat bett'nor 'im. (***DL***, Act I, Scene 1, 310: 38-9, Mrs Gascoyne.)

Note: *needs* in the first ***SL*** example is in italics in the original text.

II Conjunction *as* (for standard *that*):

I hear ***as*** Walter's got another bout on. (***OC***, Part I, 183: 22, Father)

…there's that much draught i' yon scullery, ***as*** it blows through your ribs like through a five-barred gate. (***SL***, Chapter VIII, 235: 21-2, Morel)

It's a nice thing ***as*** a man as comes home from th' pit parched up canna ha'e a drink got 'im. (***CFN***, Act I, 10: 1-2, Father)

They've been saying a long time now ***as*** that young electrician is here a bit too often. (***WH***, Act III, 98: 24-5, Grandmother)

They tell me, missus, ***as*** your mester's not hoom yet. (***WH***, Act III, 99: 27, Rigley)

'E's bin plenty of times, an' every time our Harry tells 'im ***as*** Missis won't be bothered wi' him – (***MGR***, Act I, Scene 2, 123: 36-7, Mr Hemstock)

An' I dunna wish ***as*** I'd niver seen 'er, no I dunna. (***DL***, Act I, Scene 2, 329: 1-2, Luther)

Note: The second *as* in the ***CFN*** example is not a conjunction; it is a relative pronoun – see Section VII (e).

III Definite Article *the*

III (a) reduction of definite article, usually shown as *th'*:

Did you call at ***th' 'Prince of Wales'***? (***OC***, Part II, 189: 5-6, Mrs Rigley)

You live like ***th' mice***, an' you pop out at night to see what's going on. (***SL***, Chapter I, 19: 9-10, Morel)

I mun get me weshed. We s'll ha'e ***th' men*** here directly. (***CFN***, Act I, 14: 38-9, Father)

I'll see you down ***th' line***. (***WH***, Act I, Scene 2, 77: 28, Holroyd)

'E'd only ter stick 'is 'ead out o' ***th' door***, an' 'er'd run like a pig as 'ears the bucket. (***MGR***, Act I, Scene 1, 115: 22-3, Mrs Hemstock)

Th' owd doctor's bin. He told us to ax you to see her settled down – (***MGR***, Act III, Scene 2, 166: 33-4, Harry)

It wor a haccident I got i' ***th' pit***, i' ***th' sta'*** wheer I wor workin. (***DL***, Act I, Scene 1, 304: 27-8, Joe)

III (b) omission of definite article:

If I drop a bit of bread at ***[ ]*** pit, in all the dust an' dirt, I pick it up an' eat it. (***SL***, Chapter IV, 103: 15-16 Morel)

Good Evenin', Missis! 'Asn't Carlin come? ***[ ]*** Mester up stairs? (***CFN***, Act I, 18: 27, Barker)

There's some women at ***[ ]*** New Inn, what's come from Nottingham – (***WH***, Act 1, Scene 1, 65: 13-14, Jack)

You know how it was raining. I got home from ***[ ]*** pit soaked. (***MGR***, Act III, Scene 2, 161: 15-16, Mr Wilcox)

[ ] Pump wor frozzen this mornin'. (***MGR***, Act IV, Scene 2, 171: 16, Mrs Smalley)

Wheer's my Dad?...Gone to ***[ ]*** registrar's. (***MGR***, Act IV, 171: 28-9, Harry and Mrs Smalley)

But he kep' on writin' to 'er, now an' again – an' she answered – as if she wor standin' at ***[ ]*** top of a flight of steps – (***DL***, Act I, Scene 1, 311: 31-3, Mrs Gascoyne)

IV Negatives

IV (a) negative particle -*na* attached to auxiliary verb:

I can***na*** see…I can***na*** see. (***OC***, Part I, 186: 3, 8, John)

I'll lay my fist about thy y'ead, I'm tellin' thee, if tha does***na*** stop that clatter. (***SL***, Chapter IV, 87: 16-17, Morel)

…ah'n non done so bad, I think…Tha 'as***na***, Joe, tha 'as***na*** indeed! (***CFN***, Act II, 23: 23-4, Barker and Father)

I shon***na*** [open the door]. I'll settle him. Shut thy claver. (***WH***, Act 1, Scene 2, 72: 37, Holroyd)

Tha ned***na*** but gi'e me a cat-lick. I'm as snug as a bug in a rug. (***MGR***, Act I, Scene 1, 113: 32-3, Mrs Hemstock)

Dun***na*** thee do nowt as ter'll repent of, Luther – dun***na*** thee. (***DL***, Act III, 355: 9-10, Mrs Gascoyne)

IV (b) contraction of auxiliary verb *will, have, be* with full form of negative (*not*), rather than as *won't, isn't, haven't* etc:

I know he***'ll not*** go to work to-morrow after this! (***OC***, Part I, 187: 40, Elizabeth Bates)

Is he drunk?...No! No – he***'s not***! He – he's asleep. (***OC***, Part II, 195: 34-5, Annie and Elizabeth Bates)

Th' gaffer come down to our stall this morning, an' 'e says: 'You know, Walter, this 'ere ***'ll not*** do…' (***SL***, Chapter I, 25: 24-5, Morel, quoting the pit-manager)

Our Ernest'll be in in a minute, and we***'re not*** going to have this row going on…(***CFN***, Act I, 13: 32-3, Mother)

Hasn't Ma come? I never saw her. Hello Maggie, you***'ve not*** gone yet, you see (***CFN***, Act II, 40: 15-17, Nellie Lambert)

Don't, he [the rat]'ll fly at you!...He***'ll not*** get a chance. (***WH***, Act I, Scene 2, 72: 27-8, Mrs Holroyd and Holroyd)

I***'ve not*** finished with it – but you can drink with me. – Here! (***MGR***, Act II, Scene 1, 136: 11-12, The Baker)

I allers said I'***d not*** marry one [a collier]. I'd had enough wi' my father an' th' lads. (***MGR***, Act IV, 171: 38-9, Mrs Smalley)

It's like this 'ere, Missis, if you***'ll not*** say nothink about it – sin' it's got to come out atween us. (***DL***, Act I, Scene 1, 311: 13-14, Mrs Gascoyne)

IV (c) omission of *'ll* with full form of *not*, rather than as *won't*:

He [the Baron] wants to see the Missis, an' we ***[ ]*** not let him. (***MGR***, Act 1, Scene 2, 124: 18, Mr Hemstock)

Note: See Chapter 4 for a discussion of this particular construction.

IV (d) *non* as negative marker instead of *not*:

I couldna say wheer he is – 'e's ***non*** ower theer! (***OC***, Part II, 189: 40 – 190: 1, Rigley)

'Bill,' I says, 'tha ***non*** wants them three nuts does ter? …' (***SL***, Chapter I, 15: 12-13, Morel)

Hot! It's ***non*** hot! I could do wi' it ten times hotter. (***CFN***, Act I, 14: 12-13, Father)

They've ***non*** hurt your house, have they? (***WH***, Act 1, Scene 2, 78: 39, Holroyd)

Summat's gen 'im mulligrubs. 'E'll ***non*** live long. (***MGR***, Act I, Scene 1, 114: 19, Mrs Hemstock)

Bettesworth 'ud ***non*** ha' clat-farted but for nosy Hewett. (***DL***, Act 1, Scene 1, 305: 11, Joe)

IV (e) *never* as negative marker instead of *not* (in some instances standard English would require the use of an auxiliary verb such as *do*, e.g. *I didn't see him*; *you didn't say…*; *I didn't give…*):

No, mother, I've ***never*** seen him. Why? Has he come up an' gone past to Old Brinsley? He hasn't, mother, 'cos I ***never*** saw him. (***OC***, Part I, 184: 38-9, Annie)

You ***never*** said you was coming... (***SL***, Chapter I, 12: 8, William Morel)

Oh! There now, I ***never*** gave him that rose…What a nuisance! (***CFN***, Act III, 58: 31-3, Nellie Lambert)

I bet he'll ***never*** go to work to-morrow, mother – will he? (***WH***, Act I, Scene 1, 66: 31, Jack)

Where are they? I s'd think they've ***never*** carted off an' left th' 'ouse em'py. (***MGR***, Act IV, 175: 10-11, Mrs Smalley)

They reckon I ***niver*** got it while I wor at work. (***DL***, Act I, Scene 1, 303: 27, Joe)

IV (f) more than one negative marker ('double negative' or multiple negation):

I ca***n't*** make the fire do it ***no*** faster, can I? (***OC***, Part I, 185: 27, Annie)

'Er's a bright spark, from th' look on 'er – an' one as wun***na*** do him owermuch good ***neither***. (***SL***, Chapter V, 126: 23-4, Morel)

You do***n't*** want ***no*** other woman to touch him, to wash him and lay him out, do you? (***WH***, Act III, 106: 35-7, Grandmother)

She'd ate-n the great piece of cold mutton left from yesterday, an' then said I had***n't*** left 'er ***no*** money for ***no*** meat. (***MGR***, Act III, Scene 2, 161: 22-4, Mr Wilcox)

I ***niver*** want thee to do ***nowt*** for me, ***niver no*** more. (***DL***, Act II, 333: 37, Luther)

Note: *She* in the ***MGR*** example is in italics in the original text.

V Plurals

V (a) unmarked plural of nouns of measurement after a numeral

Not ***four foot*** of space, there wasn't – yet it scarce bruised him. (***OC***, Part II, 195: 8, pit manager)

I've niver danced for ***twenty year***...(***SL***, Chapter III, 73: 26, Morel)

I want motherin', Nurse. I feel as if I could scraïght. I've been that worked-up this last ***eight month*** – (***MGR***, Act II, Scene 3, 149: 6-7, Harry)

I've said it, haven't I. There's my gal gone ***four month*** wi' childt to your Luther. (***DL***, Act I, Scene 1, 308: 37-8, Mrs Purdy)

Tha's bin an' spent ***a hundred and twenty pound*** i' four days? (***DL***, Act III, 352: 26-7, Mrs Gascoyne)

V (b) plural marking of non-count nouns:

Let's have ***our*** tea***s***, mother, should we? (***OC***, Part I, 185: 4, Annie)

The children came home from school and had ***their*** tea***s***. (***SL***, Chapter IV, 85: 24-5, Narrator)

Goodness! – I hope he'll let us get ***our*** tea***s*** first. (***CFN***, Act I, 8: 1-2, Nellie Lambert)

VI Preposition *on* (for standard *of*), usually before pronouns:

…a lot o' stuff come down atop ***'n*** 'im. (***OC***, Part II, 193: 20-1, man in pit-clothes)

Then get out ***on*** it (the house] – it's mine. Get out ***on*** it…Then ger out ***on***'t – ger out ***on***'t! (***SL***, Chapter I, 33: 8, 10, Morel)

It's you as eggs 'em on against me, both ***on*** 'em. (***CFN***, Act I, 12: 24-5, Father)

…han yer seen nowt ***on*** 'im? (***WH***, Act III, 99: 36, Rigley)

I want none ***on*** thee – go! (***MGR***, Act II, Scene 1, 141: 6, Harry)

She thought a lot ***on*** me. (***DL***, Act I, Scene 2, 329: 28-9, Luther)

VII Pronouns

VII (a) **Demonstrative** *them* (for standard *those*), both when preceding a noun (acting as determiner/demonstrative adjective) and when standing alone (demonstrative pronoun):

Mind!…Ah've said many a time as Ah'd fill up ***them ruts*** in this entry, sumb'dy 'll be breakin' their legs yit. (***OC***, Part II, 190: 26-7, Rigley)

I got these from that stall where y'ave ter get ***them marbles*** in ***them holes*** – an' I got these two in two goes… (***SL***, Chapter I, 12: 12-13, William Morel)

They gran' things ***them fountain pens***. (***CFN***, Act I, 19: 24, Carlin)

The Lord above alone knows – but I's warrant it's one o' these riotin' tricks – stopping ***them blacklegs*** as wor goin' down to see to th' roads. (***DL***, Act IV, 356: 38 - 357: 1-2, Mrs Gascoyne)

Elastic stockings! – what's ***them***? (***SL***, Chapter VI, 155: 36, Geoffrey or Maurice Leivers)

…well yer know too much then: you' wiser than ***them*** as knows, you are! (***CFN***, Act I, 10: 6-7, Father)

This is what she's been working for…Then let ***them*** as has worked be paid. (***MGR***, Act IV, 178: 4-5, Mrs Smalley and Harry)

…let ***them*** as cooked the goose eat it, that's all. – Let him arrange it hisself…(***DL***, Act I, Scene 1, 316: 36-8, Mrs Gascoyne)

VII (b) **Personal** pronouns

(i) availability of an extra pronoun, the old second person singular pronoun *thou* which is no longer found in standard English; this has subject form *thou* (usually represented as *tha*) (for standard *you*) (with reduced form *ter*), and object form *thee* (also for standard *you*):

…I shouted, 'Are ***ter*** comin', Walt?'(***OC***, Part II, 190: 7-8, Rigley)

But ***tha*** mun let me ta'e ***thee*** down [pit] sometime, an' ***tha*** can see for thysen. (***SL***, Chapter I, 19: 16-17, Morel to Gertrude Coppard)

Oh ah, I know ***tha***'ll ha'e summat ter say. (***CFN***, Act I, 14: 16, Father to Mother)

What? ***Tha*** thought ***tha***'d play thy monkey tricks on me, did ***ter***? …But I'm going to show ***thee***. (***WH***, Act II, 81: 17-19, Holroyd to Mrs Holroyd)

Tha hasna bothered thysen above thy boot-tops. (***MGR***, Act IV, 174: 20, Harry to Rachel)

Well, I s'd ha thought thy belly 'ud a browt ***thee*** whoam afore this…Doesn't ***ter*** want no dinner? (***DL***, Act I, Scene 1, 303: 10-12, Mrs Gascoyne to Joe)

(ii) use of *'er*, and sometimes *öw*, as female subject pronoun (for standard *she*). (*Öw* would seem to be a remnant of the Old English/Middle English pronoun form *heo/ho*. In the ***CFN*** example below both forms appear, use of *Öw* perhaps indicating heavier stress than *'er*.)

'Er's a bright spark, from th' look on 'er – an' one as wunna do him owermuch good neither. (***SL***, Chapter V, 126: 23-4, Morel)

'Ave you got any fresh music?...Ah, I bet ***'er*** 'as. ***Öw***'s gerrin' some iv'ry day or töw. (***CFN***, Act II, 21: 18-19, Barker and Father)

Her's locked me out. Let me smash that bloody door in. (***WH***, Act II, 81: 10-11, Holroyd)

'Er's rayther bad today, Nurse. I s'll be glad when ***'er'***s gone. (***MGR***, Act II, Scene 3, 148: 33-4, Harry)

Er wor that high an' mighty, ***'er*** wanted summat bett'nor 'im. (***DL***, Act I, Scene 1, 310: 38-9, Mrs Gascoyne)

VII (c) **Possessive** personal pronouns, including forms of second person singular pronoun *thou*

(i) when preceding a noun (acting as determiner/possessive adjective) (for standard *your*):

Nay, tha niver said thankyer for nowt i' ***thy*** life,did ter? (***SL***, Chapter I, 15: 7-8, Morel to Mrs Morel)

What? Tha thought tha'd play ***thy*** monkey tricks on me, did ter? …But I'm going to show thee. (***WH***, Act II, 81: 17-19, Holroyd to Mrs Holroyd)

Tha hasna bothered thysen above ***thy*** boot-tops. (***MGR***, Act IV, 174: 20, Harry to Rachel)

Well, I s'd ha thought ***thy*** belly 'ud a browt thee whoam afore this…Doesn't ter want no dinner? (***DL***, Act I, Scene 1, 303: 10-12, Mrs Gascoyne to Joe)

(ii) when standing alone (possessive pronoun) (for standard *his, yours, ours* etc.):

Why, what children's better looked after than ***hisn***, I sh'd like to know. (***SL***, Chapter 1, 32: 17-18, Morel)

Did they give my father's banns out?... ***Hisn*** an' ***thine***. (***MGR***, Act V, Scene 2, 184: 8-9, Rachel and Harry)

…it's nowt b'r a dirty trick o' ***his'n*** to ta'e a poor lass like my long thing, an' go an' marry a woman wi' money – (***DL***, Act I, Scene 1, 310: 18-19, Mrs Purdy)

You've a right to some compensation, an' that lass o' ***yourn*** has, but let them as cooked the goose eat it, that's all. (***DL***, Act I, Scene 1, 316: 35-7, Mrs Gascoyne)

...it's not th' bad women as 'as bastards nowadays...It's fools like ***our'n*** – poor thing. (***DL***, Act I, Scene 2, 329: 38-9, Mrs Purdy)

(iii) use of (standard) *our, your, their* as markers of kinship:

Make haste, ***our Annie.*** (***OC***, Part I, 185: 25-6, John)

They don't care how they pig it...They don't. ***Our Tom***'s just the same. (***SL***, Chapter II, 39: 36-7, Mrs Morel and Mrs Kirk)

Our Ernest'll be in in a minute, and we're not going to have this row going on... (***CFN***, Act I, 13: 32-3, Mother)

Shut up ***our Minnie***! (***WH***, Act I, Scene 1, 65: 18, Jack)

Your Susy wasn't in – I wonder what she wants. (***MGR***, Act I, Scene 2, 125: 22, The Baker)

Our Harry an' her's matched; – a pair of mealy-mouthed creeps...(***MGR***, Act I, Scene 2, 126: 24-5, Mrs Smalley)

But ***our Luther*** never went wi' ***your Bertha***. How d'you make it out? (***DL***, Act I, Scene 1, 309: 10-ll, Mrs Gascoyne)

I walked ower wi' Jim Horrocks ter ***their Annie***'s i' Mansfield. (***DL***, Act III, 345: 23-4, Luther)

VII (d) **Reflexive** personal pronouns, including forms of second person singular pronoun *thou* (for standard *myself, yourself, himself, themselves* etc.):

...if you'll just step inside an' see as th' childer doesn't come downstairs and set ***theirselves*** afire. (***OC***, Part II, 189: 18-19, Mrs Rigley)

Sluther off an' let me wesh ***my-sen***. (***SL***, Chapter I, 27: 34-5, Morel)

I mun get ***me*** weshed. We s'll ha'e th' men here directly. (***CFN*** Act I, 14: 38-9, Father)

I canna ma'e out what 'e's done wi ***'issen***. (***WH***, Act III, 99: 39, Rigley)

Tha'll happen come to lie thyself, my lad, an' then tha can think o' me hours an' hours by ***mysen***. (***MGR***, Act I, Scene 1, 119: 7-9, Mrs Hemstock)

…I fell ower your lantern and cut ***me***. (***MGR***, Act III, Scene 1, 158: 18-19, Harry)

Tha hasna bothered ***thysen*** above thy boot-tops. (***MGR***, Act IV, 174: 20, Harry to Rachel)

Let him arrange it ***hisself*** – an' if he does nothink, put him i' court, that's all. (***DL***, Act I, Scene 1, 316: 37-8, Mrs Gascoyne)

Tha pleases ***thysen***. Tha can sleep by ***thysen*** for iver, if ter's a mind to't. (***DL***, Act II, 333: 25-6, Luther)

VII (e) **Relative** pronoun *as* or *what* (for standard *who*, *which, that*):

Nay, I don't want to dance that – it's not one ***as*** I care about. (***SL***, Chapter I, 18: 30, Morel)

…you' wiser than them ***as*** knows, you are! (***CFN***: Act I, 10: 6-7, Father)

Well, what can you expect of a man ***as*** 'as been shut up i' th' pit all day? (***WH***, Act III, 98, 7-8, Grandmother)

There's some women at New Inn, ***what***'s come from Nottingham – (***WH***, Act I, Scene 1, 65: 13-14, Jack)

'E once had a rabbit ***what*** got consumption… (***MGR***, Act I, Scene 1, 115: 33-4, Mrs Hemstock)

Job Arthur's a man ***as*** can play his own tune on any mortal woman, brazen as brass or cuddlin' as a fiddle…Or like a bagpipe ***as*** wants squeezin', or a mandoline ***as*** wants tickling – he gets a tune out of the whole job lot, the whole band – (***MGR***, Act IV, 178: 33-8, Rachel)

I canna see as you're so badly off. You've got a husband ***as*** doesn't drink, ***as*** waits on you hand and foot, ***as*** gives you a free hand in everything. It's you ***as*** doesn't know when you're well off, madam. (***DL***, Act III, 349: 17-20, Mrs Gascoyne)

…it's not th' bad women ***as*** 'as bastards nowadays – they've a sight too much gumption. (***DL***, Act I, Scene 2, 329: 38-9, Mrs Purdy)

Note: The first *as* in the first ***DL*** example is not a relative pronoun; it is a conjunction – see Section II.

VIII Verb forms

VIII (a) present tense *han* (for standard *have*), usually when acting as auxiliary verb (contracted form *'n*):

What, ***han'*** yer ***knocked off***?...We ***han***, Missis. (***SL***, Chapter IV, 102: 27-8, Mrs Dakin and a collier)

'An yer ***got*** a drink for me? (***CFN***, Act I, 9: 38, Father).

Is this [rice pudding] what you ***'n had***? (***CFN***, Act I, 13: 11, Father)

Hanna you about ***done*** theer? (***WH***, Act I, Scene 2, 77: 25, Holroyd)

We ***'n got*** a new assistant. I like him better than th' owd doctor. (***MGR***, Act I, Scene 1, 122: 16-17, Mrs Hemstock)

Tha's more fondness for that goose than I ***han***, Nurse. (***MGR***, Act I, Scene 1, 121: 6-7, Mrs Hemstock)

…I ***'n got*** thee to keep on ten shillin's a wik club money, ***han*** I? (***DL***, Act I, Scene 1, 306: 13-14, Mrs Gascoyne)

VIII (b) forms of present tense with singular and plural subjects (including with *thou/ter* etc.) which follow different agreement patterns from those of standard English, the latter requiring, for example, an *–s* ending with a third person singular subject but not with a plural subject (e.g. *the children don't come*, *what do colliers want, you talk, you look*):

…if you'll just step inside an' see as ***th' childer does***n't come downstairs and set theirselves afire. (***OC***, Part II, 189: 18-19, Mrs Rigley)

Tha'rt not long in taking the curl out of me. (***SL***, Chapter I, 18: 33-4, Morel)

Eh, but ***isn't men*** great gawps! (***SL***, Chapter II, 39: 30, Mrs Kirk)

If ***tha*** oppen***s*** it [the door] again while I'm weshin' me, I'll ma'e thy jaw rattle… (***SL***, Chapter VIII, 235: 1-2, Morel)

'Bill,' ***I*** say***s***, '***tha*** non want***s*** them three nuts does ter? …' (***SL***, Chapter I, 15: 12-13, Morel)

Other men's wives bring***s*** th' panchion onto th' 'arthstone, an' get***s*** the watter for 'em… (***CFN***, Act I, 17: 25-7, Father)

An' ***tha does***na come waftin' in again when I'm weshing me, ***tha*** remember***s*** (***CFN***, Act I, 17: 39-40, Father)

Tha'rt a baffling little 'ussy. (***WH***, Act I, Scene 2, 76: 26, Holroyd)

Let me live in a street. What ***does colliers*** want livin' in country cottages, wi' nowt but fowls an' things shoutin' at you or takin' no notice of you, as if you was not there. (***MGR***, Act I, Scene 1, 116: 21-3, Mrs Hemstock)

Tha's more fondness for that goose than I han, Nurse. (***MGR***, Act I, Scene 1, 121: 6-7, Mrs Hemstock)

…tha can go wi' who ***tha*** like***s***, an' marry who ***tha*** like***s***, but if ***tha*** say***s*** a word about me, I'll come for thee. (***MGR***, Act II, Scene 1, 140: 37-9, Harry)

Tha talk***s*** like a fool, mother… ***Tha*** look***s*** like one, ma lad. (***DL***, Act I, Scene 1, 303: 30-1, Joe and Mrs Gascoyne)

I think***s*** to mysen 'It'll non become me to go an' jack up a married couple…' (***DL***, Act I, Scene 1, 310: 10-11, Mrs Purdy)

VIII (c) forms of past tense of *be*, which follow different (frequently opposite) agreement patterns from those of standard English with singular and plural subjects (e.g. *I was, he was, you were, they were* etc.):

'E wor finishin' a stint, an' th' butties 'ad gone…(***OC***, Part II, 193: 20, man in pitclothes)

Tha's niver knowed me but what I looked as if ***I wor*** goin' off in a rapid decline. (***SL***, Chapter VIII, 236: 8-9, Morel)

You never said ***you was*** coming… (***SL***, Chapter I, 12: 8, William Morel)

I know ***they*** [the grapes] ***was*** not bought for me! I know it! (***CFN***, Act III, 49: 25-6, Father)

'E wor just finishin' a stint, like, an' 'e wanted ter get it set. (***WH***, Act III, 100: 4-5, Rigley)

Dad shouts when we've gone to bed, an' thumps the table. He wouldn't if ***you was*** here. (***WH***, Act I, Scene 1, 67: 16-18, Annie)

Eh, if ***I wor*** but the staunch fourteen stone I used to be. (***MGR***, Act I, Scene 1, 117: 32-33, Mrs Hemstock)

He [the Baron] treats you as if ***you was*** dirt, an' talks like a chokin' cock – (***MGR***, Act I, Scene 2, 124: 11-12, Mr Hemstock)

…***they*** [my children] ***was*** all got of a Sunday – their father was too drunk a-Sat'day an' too tired o' wik days…(***DL***, Act I, Scene 1, 308: 20-1, Mrs Purdy)

…Missis, ***she*** [Bertha] ***wor*** better to me than iver my wife's bin. (***DL***, Act I, Scene 2, 329: 25-6, Luther)

VIII (d) forms of past tense of irregular verbs, many of which have distinct forms in standard English (e.g. *I come, I came, I have come; I see, I saw, I have seen; I blow, I blew, I have blown; I give, I gave, I have given; I fall, I fell, I have fallen; I catch, I caught, I have caught*):

…I put my bonnet on an' ***come*** straight down, Lizzie. (***OC***, Part II, 192: 4-5, Grandmother)

I shonna ***ha'e*** my ribs ***blowed*** out o' my sides wi' that draught, for nob'dy! (***SL***, Chapter II, 52: 2-3, Morel)

Th' gaffer ***come*** down to our stall this morning, an' 'e says: 'You know, Walter, this 'ere'll not do…' (***SL***, Chapter I, 25: 24-5, Morel)

Ah…I know I'm a liar. I ***knowed*** it to begin wi'. (***CFN***, Act I, 11: 21, Father)

That young electrician ***come*** knocking asking if I knew where he [Holroyd] was. (***WH***, Act III, 97: 25-6, Grandmother)

'Appen a bit o' stuff***'s fell*** an' pinned 'im. (***WH***, Act III, 100: 14-15, Rigley)

'E [Harry] ***begun*** drinkin' a bit, an' carryin' on. (***MGR***, Act I, Scene 1, 115: 17-18, Mrs Hemstock)

…it [the rabbit] died of starvation, an' 'e [Harry] ***throwed*** a hammer at me for telling him so. (***MGR***, Act I, Scene 1, 115: 35-6, Mrs Hemstock)

Summat***'s gen*** 'im mulligrubs. 'E'll non live long. (***MGR***, Act I, Scene 1, 114: 19, Mrs Hemstock)

He ***gen*** me that letter, an' says 'What's think o' that, mother?' (***DL***, Act I, Scene 1, 312: 36-7, Mrs Gascoyne)

They***'ve gave*** my mester a dirty job o' nights, at a guinea a week… (***DL***, Act I, Scene 1, 307: 9-10, Mrs Purdy)

What have you done to your head?...It wor a stone or summat ***catched*** it. It***'s gen*** me a headache. (***DL***, Act IV, 359: 28-30, Minnie and Luther)

…he got that letter when he ***com'*** whoam fra work. I ***seed*** him porin' an' porin', but I says nowt. (***DL***, Act I, Scene 1, 312: 33-5, Mrs Gascoyne)

Note: Characters are shown adopting various strategies, including: using the (standard) past participle form as a past tense (*I …come, 'e begun*); treating some verbs as though they were regular verbs and adding an *–ed* ending to the present tense form (*I knowed, 'e throwed, a stone…catched, I seed*); using a (standard) past tense or a 'regularised' *–ed* form as a past participle (*stuff's fell, They've gave, ha'e…blowed*).

VIII (e) omission of *'re* (i.e. *are* or possibly *were*), when acting either as auxiliary or as main verb (as in standard *they're coming, we're glad*)

…we ***[ ]*** com'n ter th' bottom, me an' Bower, thinkin' as 'e wor just behint us. (***OC***, Part II, 190: 8-10, Rigley)

They ***[ ]*** ta'ein' 'im ter th'ospital. (***SL***, Chapter V, 108: 20-1, pit lad)

Look you, they [the trousers] ***[ ]*** steaming like a sweating hoss (***CFN***, Act I, 11: 17-18, Father)

They ***[ ]*** commin'! (***WH***, Act III, 104: 8, Rigley)

You ***[ ]*** not thinkin of it [going to Australia], are you? (***DL***, Act III, 344: 5, Mrs Gascoyne)

…we ***[ ]*** glad t'ave yer [home]. (***SL***, Chapter XIII, 422: 27, Minnie, the maid)

…well yer know too much then: you ***[']*** wiser than them as knows, you are! (***CFN***, Act I, 10: 6-7, Father)

They ***[ ]*** gran' things them fountain pens. (***CFN***, Act I, 19: 24, Carlin)

Hello our Ernest, you ***[ ]*** home (***CFN***, Act III, 57: 19-20, Nellie Lambert)

You ***[ ]*** married now, lad, an' you canna please yoursen. (***DL***, Act I, Scene 2, 329: 14-15, Mrs Purdy)

You'll non go gettin' yourselves into trouble…We ***[ ]*** in trouble enow. (***DL***, Act III, 351: 30-1, Mrs Gascoyne and Luther)

3 Pronunciation patterns (compared with 'Received Pronunciation')

Representation of dialect pronunciation in written dialogue is a complex matter. There is no consistent matching of letters to sounds in the English spelling system, and there are no agreed conventions available to writers of dialogue in stories, novels and plays who wish to use ordinary spelling to represent the sound of natural speech. They must to some extent construct their own approximations of the sounds they wish to convey. Their difficulties may be increased when the dialogue in question involves dialect, since it introduces the complications of social class difference outlined earlier (see Chapter 1). Lawrence, therefore, had to balance a desire for authenticity in the 'sound' of his working class characters' speech with the need for basic comprehension and, indeed, tolerance on the part of what was inevitably a predominantly middle class readership. (The kinds of issues involved are considered in Chapter 7 of Hillier, 2004, which examines the spelling choices made by one particular writer. Fred Wetherill, however, was writing for 'local' readers who would immediately recognise the environment in which his story took place and also the form and sound of the language in which it was written.)

Lawrence makes some attempt to give explicit indications of local pronunciation in his spelling, particularly by fairly liberal use of the apostrophe to indicate lack of the sound /h/. Even here, however, we find rather more uses of the letter *h* than are entirely authentic. Many of the most characteristic pronunciation features are not, in fact, suggested at all in the spelling, and this may particularly apply to vowels.

The following pages, therefore, set out some of the most significant pronunciation patterns found in the dialect of Eastwood and the Erewash Valley, when compared with those of 'Received Pronunciation' (RP). Some phonetic symbols have been used in presenting this framework, but they are supplemented by 'ordinary spelling' representations and descriptions of speech sounds (see Appendix 1) for the benefit of those readers who are unfamiliar with phonetics.

Examples of relevant words are given, showing some of the ways (if any) in which Lawrence attempts to represent those sounds.

I Consonants

I (a) The **sound /h/** is not a natural part of the Erewash Valley dialect. The basic presumption, therefore, is that it will not be pronounced. There is variation, however, in the way potential /h/ words (i.e. in RP) are actually dealt with by Lawrence.

(i) sometimes an apostrophe is used:

'Asn't, 'e, 'ome, 'ad, 'is, 'alf (***OC***, Part II, 189: 4-5, Mrs Rigley)

'e, 'is, 'ead (***SL***, Chapter IV, 89: 23, Morel)

'asna (***CFN***, Act II, 23: 24, Father)

'appen, 'ere, 'ussy (***WH***, Act I, Scene 2, 76: 5, 24, 26, Holroyd)

'E, 'is, 'er, ' im, 'ead, 'as, 'ears, 'erself, 'ae'-porth (***MGR***, Act I, Scene 1, 115: 3, 6-7, 9-10, 13, 17-19, 22-4, 26-7, 29, 31, 33-5, Mrs Hemstock)

'er, 'ere, 'e, 'im (***DL***, Act I, Scene 1, 311: 4, 7, 13, 17-19, 22, 25, 28, 32, 36, Mrs Gascoyne)

(ii) sometimes no apostrophe is used:

E's just gone for 'alf an 'our afore bed-time. (***OC***, Part II, 189: 4-5, Mrs Rigley)

Er wor that high an' mighty, 'er wanted summat bett'nor 'im. (***DL***, Act I, Scene 1, 310: 38-9, Mrs Gascoyne)

Er does as 'er likes (***DL***, Act III, 353: 20, Luther)

(iii) sometimes the letter *h* is used:

heered, him, he, half, (***OC***, Part I, 183: 25-6, Father)

his, ***hisn*** (***SL***, Chapter I, 32: 17 (quoting Mrs Morel), 18, Morel)

home, ***ha'e*** (***CFN***, Act I, 10: 1-2, Father)

hear, hurt, ***house***, ***have*** (***WH***, Act I, Scene 2, 78: 12, 39, Holroyd)

Hisn, having (***MGR***, Act V, Scene 2, 184: 9, 27, Harry)

he, how, hundred, his sen (***DL***, Act I, Scene 1, 307: 4, 17, 22, 26, 34, Mrs Gascoyne)

(iv) sometimes a speaker introduces an 'unnecessary' /h/ sound (possibly 'hypercorrects'), usually when applied to a stressed item:

Ah'd a ta'en a ***hoath*** as 'e wor just behint…(***OC***, Part II, 190: 10, Rigley)

Tired – I ***ham*** that…*You* don't know what it is to be tired, as *I'm* tired. (***SL***, Chapter II, 46: 32-3, Morel)

I'm too tired ter ***h'eat***. (***CFN***, Act I, 12: 15, Father)

Well I never! I ***ham*** surprised, I can tell you – (***MGR***, Act V, Scene 1, 181: 18-19, Mr Wilcox)

An' thinks I, she's a ***horphan***, if she's got money, an' nobbut her husband i' th' world. (***DL***, Act I, Scene 1, 310: 14-15, Mrs Purdy)

Note: *You* and *I'm* in the ***SL*** example appear in italics in the original text.

I (b) **suffix '-ing'** is pronounced as **/ɪn/**, where RP would have /ɪN/ (as in the single sound after /s/ in 's<u>ing</u>').

(i) this is usually represented as *–in'*:

finishin', comin', thinkin', breakin', frettin' (***OC***, Part II, 190: 6-7, 9, 27, 33, Rigley)

sneezin', ta'ein', cadin', darlin', runnin', slivin', nibblin' (***SL***, Chapter IV, 89: 21, 24, 31, 32, 40, Morel)

orderin', turnin' (***CFN***, Act I, 12: 29, Father)

puttin', goin' (***WH***, Act I, Scene 2, 79: 15, 28, 34, Holroyd)

shiverin', hummin', kissin', cuddlin', swimmin', rubbin', leavin', darlin', makin's, ormin' (***MGR***, Act I, Scene 1, 120: 1-2, 16, 17, 21, 26, 29, 31, 40, Mrs Hemstock)

marryin', overbearin', thinkin', havin', writin', standin', doin', mormin' (***DL***, Act I, Scene 1, 311: 4, 7, 18, 20, 29, 32-3, 35-6, Mrs Gascoyne)

(ii) though sometimes as '-ing':

beginning (***OC***, Part II, 192: 40, Grandmother)

coming (***SL***, Chapter I, 12: 8, William Morel)

steaming, sweating (***CFN***, Act I, 11: 17, Father)

bringing, hitting, coaxing, managing, ravishing, telling (***WH***, Act III, 99: 6, 13, 15, 19, 25, Grandmother)

cunning (***MGR***, Act I, Scene 1, 120: 16, Mrs Hemstock)

planting (***DL***, Act III, 345: 26, Mrs Gascoyne)

I (c) A <u>reduced</u>, or apparently <u>omitted</u>, **definite article** is usually indicated in speech via use of a **glottal stop [ʔ]** (a momentary 'stop' in the vocal tract) <u>not</u> by /t/.

Alternatively, a reduced definite article may be indicated by use of an unvoiced ‘th’ (**[θ]**) (as in ‘thing’) before a vowel sound. Actual written representation is usually via ***th’***, but the article may be omitted all together (see the examples under III (a) and (b) under ‘Grammatical patterns’ in Chapter 2).

II Vowels

(for polysyllabic words in the illustrative examples the relevant syllable is underlined)

II (a) **/a/** (a short ‘a’, as in ‘bad’) is pronounced where RP would have /A:/ (a long ‘ah’, as in ‘bard’ or the first syllable of ‘father’) in words represented as:

glass (***OC***, Part II, 192: 1, Grandmother);
dance (***SL***, Chapter I, 18: 21, 30, Morel);
draughtin’, waftin’ (***CFN***, Act I, 17: 18, 39, Father);
blasted (***WH***, Act II, 81: 14, Holroyd);
laughing (***MGR***, Act I, Scene 1, 113: 23, Mrs Hemstock)
bastards (***DL***, Act I, Scene 2, 329: 38, Mrs Purdy)

II (b) **/Y/** (a short ‘oo’, as in ‘put’) is pronounced where RP would have /ς/, as in ‘putt’, in words represented as:

trouble, butties, stuff (***OC***, Part II, 192: 24, Grandmother; 193: 20, man in pit-clothes)
dust, snuff, shoves, duckey, dost, runnin’, up, but (***SL***, Chapter I, 47: 8, and Chapter IV, 89: 22, 23, 27, 31, 32, Morel)
summat, mun (***CFN***, Act I, 14: 16, 38, Father)

bloody*, *monkey (***WH***, Act II, 81: 11, 18, Holroyd)

drunk, , mother, rough, touch, money (***MGR***, Act II, Scene 3, 148: 28, 30, 31, 37, 38, Harry)

done, money, does, comfortable, enough, trustin', gumption (***DL***, Act I, Scene 2, 329: 7-8, 18, 30, 32, 34-6, 39, Mrs Purdy)

Note: Lawrence does try occasionally to give some indication of this sound: see ***sumb'dy*** (***OC***, Part II, 190: 27, Rigley), ***munny*** (***DL***, Act I, Scene 1, 303: 17, Joe), ***cunjurin'*** (***DL***, Act I, Scene 1, 305: 6, Joe), ***cumpany*** (***DL***, Act I, Scene 1, 307: 11, Mrs Purdy), to represent the sound of 'somebody', 'money', 'conjuring', 'company'; see too Morel's mocking attempt to echo his wife's apparent pronunciation of 'nothing' as ***nathing*** (***SL***, Chapter II, 52: 40), and Holroyd's comparable mockery of Blackmore with his repeated ***calamniating*** (***WH***, Act II, 83: 38-40).

II (c) **[a:]** (rather like a 'lengthened' short 'a', as in something like 'baat') is pronounced where RP would have /Au/, as in 'bout', in words represented as:

downstairs (***OC***, Part II, 189: 19, Mrs Rigley)

brown, mouse (***SL***, Chapter IV, 89: 19, 32, Morel)

'ow*, *now (***CFN***, Act I, 19: 16, Father)

out, our, outside, about, now (***WH***, Act I, Scene 1, 65: 3, 16, 18, 23, 27, 33, 37, Jack)

'ouse*, *proud, our (***MGR***, Act IV, 175: 11, 34, 39, Mrs Smalley)

pound (***DL***, Act III, 352: 26, Mrs Gascoyne)

Note: Lawrence makes very frequent use of the spelling ***tha*** to represent the sound of 'thou' (e.g. ***CFN***, Act II, 23: 24, Father).

II (d) **[ei]** is frequently pronounced (as in 'pay' and 'day') where RP would have /i:/ (as in 'pea' and 'tea'), especially in *we* followed by (contracted) *han*, represented as:

We'n got a new assistant. (***MGR,*** Act I, Scene 1, 122: 16-17, Mrs Hemstock)

...Now Nurse, thee read it [the will]. ***We***'n all read. Now thee read it. (***MGR***, Act IV, 177: 38-9, Harry)

Thy wire! Dost mean a tallygram? No, ***we***'n had nowt. (***DL***, Act III, 342: 8-9, Mrs Gascoyne)

but see the attempted representation of the 'ay' sound in 'eaten' in:

An' has ter ***aten*** owt? (***SL***, Chapter XIII, 418: 12, Morel)

She'd ***ate-n*** the great piece of cold mutton left from yesterday... (***MGR***, Act III, Scene 2, 161: 22-3, Mr Wilcox)

...I've ***aten*** my dinner, a'most. (***DL***, Act I, Scene 1, 306: 10, Joe)

and especially the heavily stressed *thee*, frequently represented as ***thaïgh***:

What are ***thaïgh*** doin' 'ere? (***WH***, Act II, 82: 30, Holroyd)

Does ***thaïgh*** like roast pork? (***MGR***, Act I, Scene 1, 117: 28, Mrs Hemstock)

What's ***thaïgh*** got ter do wi' it? (***MGR***, Act II, Scene 2, 146: 12, Mrs Smalley)

II (e) **[ə] (**as in the final syllable of 'mother'), for unstressed vowels in words like 'to', 'into', 'you', you're, and the reduced form of 'thou', is represented as:

Are ***ter*** comin', Walt?... so we com'n ***ter*** th' bottom… (***OC***, Part II, 190: 7-9, Rigley)

…he [Taffy] slives up and shoves 'is 'ead on ***yer***…I wor just in time ***ter*** get 'im [the mouse] by th' tail. (***SL***, Chapter IV, 89: 23, 34, Morel)

Yer at me again, are ***yer***? I've had about enough on't. (***SL***, Chapter II, 58: 25-6, Morel)

…'e seems to be goin' on nicely, thank ***yer***…I want ***ter*** get back… (***CFN***, Act I, 18: 31, 38-9, Barker)

Arena ***ter*** goin' ***ter*** get me öwt for it? (***WH***, Act I, Scene 2, 78: 21-2, Holroyd)

…I'm thy spittoon, tha can spit owt in***ter*** me. (***MGR***, Act II, Scene 1, 139: 15-16, Harry)

My mother worna one ***ter*** handle you very tender…(***MGR***, Act II, Scene 3, 148: 30, Harry)

It sends ***yer*** that thin an' threadbare, y'have ***ter*** stop sometime. (***DL***, Act I, Scene 1, 308: 4, Joe)

4 'Real' – i.e. naturally-occurring – examples of grammatical features presented in Chapter 2

A large majority of the features in the framework presented in Chapter 2 can be found in my own data. Examples of each of these are set out below. (Many of those which have not yet appeared in my data are nevertheless familiar to me from my own childhood and youth. I even find myself using one or two of them occasionally!)

The principal source of these 'real' examples has been the tape recordings (and the notes kept at the time) made by me between 1991 and 1993 of conversations with and between primary school children – 'infants' (aged between 5 and 6) and 'juniors' (aged between 9 and 11). The recordings were made in either a classroom or 'quiet room' setting. Some of the conversations involved children talking to me, but most had children in groups of three talking to each other as they co-operated in playing educational games on the computer. The computer games for the infants included Fantasy That!, Granny's Garden and Oz, and those for the juniors included 'quest'-type games such as Space Mission Mada, Nature Park Adventure, Mapventure and Zillion. The latter games required the children to perform tasks and/or collect objects of various kinds. (I had already found such computer games to be a useful focus for the recording of rich conversational data involving small groups of children, including my own two sons, when collecting material for my Ph.D thesis – see Hillier, 1992.)

Most of the examples quoted come from Devonshire Drive Juniors (***DDJ***), with a very few from Devonshire Drive Infants (***DDI***) and Greasley Beauvale Infants (***GBI***). The imbalance arises partly because the games for the juniors were inevitably more complex and challenging than the ones for the infants, and generated much more consultation, and partly from the fact that the older children tended in any case to be much more talkative. Collection of the junior data alone over the two years involved 23 different children, boys and girls, seven of whom participated more than once. The ***DDJ*** examples dated '30/6/92' are taken from a long conversation I had with two of the boys on that day; this covered a wide range of topics, all introduced by them, including swimming, golf, football, music lessons, and their experiences in school and at home.

The children's examples are supplemented by field notes (***FN***), that is, verbatim notes written 'on the hoof' of short contributions to conversations heard and overheard in the area over the years. Some names have been changed. Two additional sources are: a retired miner, interviewed in Mansfield by Brian Johnston as part of a 'Down Your Way' programme broadcast on BBC Radio 4 on 22 February 1987; an issue of the *Nottingham Evening Post* dated 11 August 2008, which celebrated the success of a young Mansfield woman, Rebecca Adlington, in the 2008 Olympic Games in Beijing.

The actual form of presentation of these spoken examples raises many questions – the kinds of questions and difficulties probably faced by Lawrence, and discussed at the beginning of Chapter 3, but in an even more complex and heightened form. These are, after all, samples of real, spontaneous, speech transcribed into written form. They are not, as in Lawrence, samples of written language which is intended to give the appearance of real speech, and which is, furthermore, intended to be read as though 'heard' in a particular way. (Chapter 1 of Hillier, 2004 discusses the many different strands involved in the apparently 'simple' spoken v. written language dichotomy.) These examples are, too, even more 'out of context' than the Lawrence examples, which readers can easily trace back to their original literary source if desired. How can these snippets be made as meaningful as necessary for present purposes? The transcribing of naturally-occurring spoken language of any kind is not without its difficulties, particularly where several participants – and varying degrees of background noise – may be involved, as in the children's recordings. (It is not always possible, for example, to distinguish between individual boys' and girls' voices, though for present purposes this has not been regarded as a significant factor.) In these specific examples reference may be made to entities in the immediate environment which are not always obvious, and these have to be explained, where possible, to the reader. Some may be unclear even to the transcriber and may have to be guessed at or remain obscure. In the examples presented here, however, all the important detail – especially the grammatical feature under discussion – is clear and unambiguous.

The following are the general principles which have been adopted for transcribing these short examples of spoken language:

- clarifications of reference are placed in square brackets, e.g. *it* [*the robot*], *it* [*the pencil?*];
- there is minimal use of conventional punctuation marks, such as upper case letters, full stops and commas, the main exception being the use of upper case for proper names;
- there is occasional use of question and exclamation marks;
- apostrophes are used for conventional contractions, e.g. *can't, we're*;
- brief pauses are signalled by the use of a dash;
- omitted words are signalled by the use of three dots (...);
- any uncertainties of transcription are placed within round brackets, e.g. *must be (nearly as big as) Bishop Street.*

We come then to the question of how these examples should be read – or rather 'heard'. How far can the ordinary conventions of written language be used to convey the authentic 'sound' of these samples of real speech by real (as distinct from fictional) individuals? Should an attempt be made to follow Lawrence's approximate system but to apply it rather more consistently? How can the manner of presentation avoid an appearance of stereotypical mimicry, even caricature? How can the examples be made as comprehensible as possible to readers of all social, regional and even national backgrounds? Is special treatment of any kind in fact necessary at all, given that the separate examples come from essentially the 'same' linguistic environment? (Unlike Lawrence, I am not trying to distinguish between the speech of different characters.) Furthermore, the examples have been chosen to illustrate specifically grammatical, rather than pronunciation, features and the overall patterns of the latter have already been established in Chapter 3.

What follows is a compromise. Most of the conventions of ordinary written language have been regarded as adequate for present purposes and there has been little or no attempt to convey by visual means the characteristic 'sound' of these examples. Readers are asked to accept the basic working premise that the pronunciation patterns set out in Chapter 3 apply for each quoted example unless specifically indicated, and that this is so for both consonants and vowels. The apostrophe has not been used to signal either lack of /h/ or suffix 'in': the letter *h* should be regarded as merely a visual symbol, the presumption being that *h* is ignored in speech (/h/ should not be sounded); suffix *-ing* should be sounded as 'in'. 'Definite meaning' which is indicated via apparent 'omission' of the definite article, shown under III (b) as ***[ ]***, is realised by use of a glottal stop (see Appendix 1). So far as vowels are concerned, the pattern is as presented in Chapter 3, with the single exception that the /i:/ vowel should always be heard as in 'pea', and not as in the older and now rarer form 'pay' (see Section II (d) of Chapter 3). Unstressed vowels in *you* and *em* (representing unstressed *them*) should be heard as [ə] (compare Lawrence's *yer*). The *tha* in VII (b)(i) and VII (c)(i) is as given in Section II (c) of Chapter 3 and follows Lawrence's spelling in representing the sound of 'thou'; the unstressed vowel in *thy* in the same example should be heard as something like 'thi' – as in 'this' without the final 's'.

Examples have been placed under the heading for the relevant grammatical feature, and the headings follow precisely the same order and numbering system as in Chapter 2. The examples are highlighted in exactly the same way, i.e. via the use of bold italics for the non-standard form being cited or the brackets used to mark the site of an 'omitted' item. Source and date, plus brief contextual information where necessary, are given for each example. Additional comments on two of the features represented will be found in the closing paragraphs of this chapter.

I Adverbs

I (a) without –ly:

I pressed that one [key] ***wrong*** but it [the robot] went up (***DDJ***, 26/11/91)

you can go dead ***quick*** (***DDJ***, 24/3/92)

get that – get that ***quick***...get that triangle ***quick*** (***DDJ***, 24/3/92)

II Conjunction *as* (for standard that):

...while we're training the birds we show the hen to the cock – this gives them the idea they know ***as*** when they come off a race...the hen's waiting for em... (BBC Radio 4, 22/2/87, retired miner, 60s)

III Definite article *the*

III (b) omission of definite article:

most people think it [the name Sarah] hasn't got a H on ***[ ]*** end and it has (***DDJ***, 26/11/91)

[ ] tape's stopped! (***DDJ***, 10/3/92)

if you get in ***[ ]*** middle it probably will - you'll probably hit it [the ball] wide of ***[ ]*** hole (***DDJ***, 30/6/92)

I go [to Selston] with my uncle – in ***[ ]*** car (***DDJ***, 30/6/92)

you know the man up at ***[ ]*** top who watches you go down…he come down blowing ***[ ]*** whistle – down ***[ ]*** slide – with his shorts and tee shirt on (***DDJ***, 30/6/92)

then he got on ***[ ]*** floor and he says that I'd punched him in his face (***DDJ***, 30/6/92)

IV Negatives

IV (c) omission of *'ll* with full form of *not*, rather than as *won't*:

it [the number to be entered] ***[ ]*** not be the same (***DDJ***, 24/3/92)

there ***[ ]*** not be one there so you may as well just go on the bottom row or any rows (***DDJ***, 24/3/92)

you ***[ ]*** not bodge it up – it don't matter… (***DDJ***, 24/3/92)

it [the tape] ***[ ]*** not run out cos of talking (***DDJ***, 24/3/92)

it [the bus]'ll be all right there [in the car park] Jim ***[ ]*** not it (***FN***, 19/4/94, bus driver, male, 50s?)

they could paint it [the window frame] white so it ***[ ]*** not show (***FN***, 30/9/98, woman, 80s)

you'll 'ave spotted dick ***[ ]*** not you (***FN***, 10/10/04, woman, 60s, considering menu) that [the door] ***[ ]*** not move that ***[ ]*** not (***FN***, 4/1/06, window cleaner, male, 30s/40s?)

it [the wire] ***[ ]*** not come any more… (***FN***, 10/3/06, gas fitter, male, 40s?, trying to move aside radio speaker in order to get at gas fire)

I thought I'd be getting free texts [on mobile phone] but I ***[ ]*** not (***FN***, 26/10/07, woman, 60s)

you ***[ ]*** not get a pushchair on duck (***FN***, 27/11/07, bus driver, male, 50s?)

IV (f) more than one negative marker ('double negative' or multiple negation):

you ca***n't*** have ***nothing*** there [in that place in the game] (***DDJ***, 10/3/92)

I do***n't*** want that [shape] ***neither***…I want that triangle… (***DDJ***, 24/3/92)

I'm ***not*** going to bet ***no*** more (***DDJ***, 24/3/92)

don't get the green triangles – go back – ***don't*** get ***none*** of them (***DDJ***, 24/3/92)

there ***not*** be ***no*** reduction for a group party (***FN***, 8/7/06, woman, 60s, re possible holiday booking)

it do***n't*** make ***no*** difference if you press your lever [on the coach seat] (***FN***, 10/8/08, woman, 60s)

V Plurals

V (a) unmarked plurals of nouns of measurement after a numeral:

if it goes in water then that's ***five pound*** down drain (***DDJ***, 30/6/92)

I got my full set of golf clubs for ***a hundred and twenty-seven pound*** – that's just the clubs – then I spent about another ***hundred pound*** on my bag and tees and all that (***DDJ***, 30/6/92)

she [my Mum] grounded me for about ***three week*** (***DDJ***, 30/6/92)

my brother paper rounds there – he gets ***three pound*** (***DDJ***, 26/11/91)

VI Preposition *on* (for standard *of*), usually before pronouns:

when there were three ***on*** you working at pit it'd be a fight for hot water…(BBC Radio 4, 22/2/87, retired miner, 60s)

I've seen nowt ***on*** you for about three week (***FN***, 10/11/90, man, 50s?)

if we live long enough we shall have done all ***on*** em [i.e. the lakes in the Lake District] (***FN***, 8/10/06, woman, 60s)

VII Pronouns

VII (a) **Demonstrative** *them* (for standard *those*), both when preceding a noun (acting as determiner/demonstrative adjective) and when standing alone (demonstrative pronoun):

follow ***them squiggly lines*** (***DDJ***, 10/3/92)

it's that man where you have to catch all ***them tiles*** (***DDJ***, 24/3/92)

you can get all ***them shapes*** (***DDJ***, 24/3/92)

I've gone with ***them*** [shapes] with blotches on (***DDJ***, 4/2/92)

65p – 50 - one of ***them*** and one of ***them***… (***DDJ***, 24/3/92)

don't get the green triangles – go back – don't get none of ***them*** (***DDJ***, 24/3/92)

VII (b) **Personal** pronouns

(i) availability of second person singular pronoun *thou*, with subject form *thou* (for standard *you*), and object form *thee* (for standard *you*):

tha's got thy choppers in Win! (***FN***, 4/6/88, nurse, female, early 20s?)

Note: I have followed Lawrence here in spelling 'thou' as *tha*

VII (c) **Possessive** personal pronouns, including forms of second person singular pronoun *thou*

(i) when preceding a noun (acting as determiner/possessive adjective) (for standard *your*):

tha's got ***thy*** choppers in Win! (***FN***, 4/6/88, nurse, female, early 20s?)

(ii) when standing alone (possessive pronoun) (for standard *yours*):

is that [tape recorder] ***yourn***? (***DDI***, 29/10/91)

it [your garden] must be (nearly as big as) Bishop Street then - ***yourn*** (***DDJ***, 30/6/92)

(iii) use of (standard) *our* as marker of kinship:

me and ***our David*** sat outside talking… (***FN***, 10/8/08, woman, 60s) when I went to ***our William***'s 60th [birthday party] a lot of people took a bottle of wine (***FN***, 15/8/08, woman 60s)

Our Becky has got gold! ***Our Becky*** breaks a 48-year GB duck (*Nottingham Evening Post* headlines, 11/8/08)

VII (d) **Reflexive** personal pronouns (for standard *yourself, himself*):

…just go where my finger is - - just move ***yoursen*** like that… (***DDJ***, 4/2/92)

he served ***hisself*** right (***DDI***, 8/10/91)

VII (e) **Relative** pronoun *as* or *what* (for standard *who, which, that*):

it wasn't the picture ***what*** it showed me (***DDJ***, 26/11/91)

there's…some scales and some pedals all on the sheet ***what*** you have to play… (***DDJ***, 30/6/92)

then the box ***what*** the game was in he kicked it in and ripped all board and all that lot (***DDJ***, 30/6/92)

it [the swimming pool]'s got a slide ***what*** goes about twenty metres (***DDJ***, 30/6/92)

VIII Verb forms

VIII (b) forms of present tense with singular and plural subjects, including with *thou*, which follow different agreement patterns from those of standard English; the latter requires, e.g., an *–s* ending with a third person singular subject but not with a plural subject (e.g. *tricks stand out…*):

hey - where ***'s the triangles***? (***DDJ***, 24/3/92)

there's ***one or two*** [tricks] what stand***s*** out in my mind… (BBC Radio 4, 22/2/87, retired miner, 60s)

tha's got thy choppers in Win! (***FN***, 4/6/88, nurse, female, early 20s?)

VIII (c) forms of past tense of *be*, which follow different (frequently opposite) agreement patterns from those of standard English with singular and plural subjects such as *it was, we were*:

it were about quarter past twelve (***DDJ***, 26/11/91)

I were about eight when I started getting interested [in golf] (***DDJ***, 30/6/92)

when ***I were*** in infants I used to go round punching people for nothing (***DDJ***, 30/6/92)

all of a sudden ***he were*** laughing his head off...(***DDJ***, 30/6/92)

there ***was*** lots and lots of bear***s*** (***GBI***, 10/12/91)

we was playing cricket – ***we was both*** in bat – they kept coming round and pushing us... (***DDJ***, 30/6/92)

the pit ponie***s was*** up the roads...fetching the coal... (***FN***, 22/2/87, retired miner, 60s)

...the field where all them cow***s was***, what Mary didn't like....(***FN***, 10/8/08, woman, 60s)

VIII (d) forms of past tense of irregular verbs, many of which have distinct forms in standard English (e.g. *I come, I came, I have come*; *I break, I broke, I have broken; I see, I saw, I have seen; I fall, I fell, I have fallen; I fight, I fought, I have fought*):

somebody ***come*** with an axe to kill him off and the hawks attacked him and saved him...but he still died... (***DDJ***, 30/6/92)

you know the man up at top who watches you go down...he ***come*** down blowing whistle – down slide – with his shorts and tee shirt on (***DDJ***, 30/6/92)

I ***seen*** somebody else doing it [playing the game] (***DDJ***, 29/10/91)

I ***'ve broke*** it [the pencil?] (***GBI***, 12/11/91)

right - ***have*** you ***wrote*** this down? (***DDJ***, 26/11/91)

that thing would ***have fell*** off the edge (***DDJ***, 24/3/92)

follow straight road through Brinsley then turn up - I ***'ve forgot*** what road it is – it's a big hill (***DDJ***, 30/6/92)

I ***'ve fighted*** him before (***DDJ***, 30/6/92)

I had your number in my phone when we did that walk and I ***'ve*** never ***took*** it out (***FN***, 10/8/08, woman, 60s)

Note: It will be seen that speakers use a number of different strategies, including the (standard) past participle form used as a past tense form (*I come, I seen*), the (standard) past tense form used as a past participle (*I've broke, I've forgot*), the addition of an *–ed* ending to the present tense form to create something like a 'regular' past participle (*I've fighted*).

VIII (e) omission of *'re* (i.e. *are* or possibly *were*), when acting either as auxiliary or as main verb (as in standard *they're saying, we're Ladbrokes*):

right – how much ***[ ]*** you betting on the next one? (***DDJ***, 24/3/92)

when I watch telly when I'm grounded I…sit right next to screen listening to what they ***[ ]*** saying (***DDJ***, 30/6/92)

they ***[ ]*** retiring them about fifty and some at forty six they tell me…(BBC Radio 4, 22/2/87, retired miner, 60s)

I said to him we ***[ ]*** not going to get anything to eat until…. (***FN***, 13/7/08, woman, 60s)

you don't really need to chip on the putting greens cos all you do is use your putter cos they ***[ ]*** not very far apart the holes (***DDJ***, 30/6/92)

One pound five – yeah we ***[ ]*** still in profit we ***[ ]*** still in profit – we ***[ ]*** Ladbrokes (***DDJ***, 24/3/92)

they ***[ ]*** one of the best – they ***[ ]*** some of the best defenders and he [Clough]'s going to lose them all (***DDJ***, 30/6/92, discussing Nottingham Forest football team and their manager)

we ***[ ]*** out this way [in this part of the countryside] on Wednesday (***FN***, 14/10/07, woman, 50s)

Two of the above features may require comment.

The first involves the omission of auxiliary *'ll,* with the full form of *not*, as provided for in the framework under IV (c). There are very many examples of this construction in my data whereas only one has been found (so far) in Lawrence: *He wants to see the Missis, an' we* ***[ ] not*** *let him* (***MGR***, Act I, Scene 2). Lawrence does, however, have several instances of contracted *'ll* with *not*, as under IV (b), for example: '*You know, Walter, this 'ere* ***'ll not*** *do…*' (***SL***, Chapter I). The reasons for this disparity are unclear. Omission would seem to be part of a general tendency towards increased economy in informal speech where circumstances – both linguistic and social – allow it (contraction from *will* to *'ll* is already an instance of this). The single ***MGR*** example appears to show Lawrence representing this tendency. The need for comprehension could have been a factor in leading him to be more explicit (i.e. by including *'ll*), but such considerations seem not to have deterred him from representing omitted *'re*. There are many examples of this latter feature under VIII (e), including Mrs Gascoyne's *You* ***[ ]*** *not thinkin of it, are you?* (***DL***, Act III), which has some, though not all, parallels with omission of *'ll*. Further research is required here!

My final comments concern the use of *tha* - as in VII (b)(i) – which has already been mentioned as being of particularly significance in Lawrence's work (see Chapter 1).

The second person singular pronoun can still be heard in parts of England, but its natural and spontaneous use in Eastwood and district is, in my experience, rare. The single example quoted above is the only one (so far) in my data and it may therefore benefit from a little explanation. The young woman speaking was a student nurse in a hospital ward in Nottingham. She was attending to a very elderly and increasingly infirm patient, and she had pulled the curtains around the bed to ensure privacy. Her *tha's got thy choppers* [i.e. teeth] *in Win!* could be clearly heard from the other side of the curtain. It was a warm and gentle exclamation as she prepared to wash her patient. The nurse told me later, when I asked, that use of *tha* had just come naturally to her in the circumstances: she and her family were from Heanor, and her grandfather always used *tha* when addressing her. The patient receiving this tender and intimate care was my mother.

Appendix 1: Selective glossary of Standard English grammatical and other terms used in frameworks

adjectives express some quality of a **noun** (e.g. *a long day, the bright sun*)

adverbs modify verbs or adjectives in some way; saying something about the action or process expressed by a **verb** (e.g. *she ran quickly*), or increasing or diminishing the quality expressed by an adverb or **adjective** (e.g. *very quickly*, *rather tall*)

agreement when two grammatical elements show that they are linked with each other by use of some kind of formal marking, such as an added **suffix** to show agreement between a singular **subject** and a singular **verb** in the present **tense** (e.g. *day dawns, the cat stretches*)

auxiliary verbs are subsidiary to, and act in concert with, main **verbs** (e.g. *she is laughing, I have run the marathon, do you take sugar?*)

conjunctions link different parts of sentences together: equal parts being linked by 'coordinating conjunctions' such as *and*, *but*, *or* etc. (e.g. *he is very tall and he walks very quickly*), and unequal parts by a wide range of 'subordinating conjunctions', including *that* (e.g. *he said that he was cold*)

consonants v. vowels individual vowels are produced by a combination of air from the lungs passing over vibrating vocal chords, the position of the tongue in different parts of the mouth, and the rounding or spreading of lips; individual consonants use different combinations of lips, teeth, tongue and parts of the vocal tract to control the passage of air; those consonants produced with vibrating vocal chords are called '**voiced consonants**', and those produced with non-vibrating vocal chords are called '**unvoiced consonants**'. Examples of words using voiced v. unvoiced consonants in comparable environments are: *bat* v. *pat*, *den* v. *ten, van* v. *fan, this* v. *thistle, that* v. *thatch*. (To hear, and feel, the difference between 'voiced' and 'unvoiced', put thumb and forefinger on either side of the larynx (Adam's apple) and pronounce each pair of words very slowly indeed, each segment at a time, as if helping a child to read. First form, and feel the effect of, the initial consonant – a perceptible movement in the larynx will occur with a voiced consonant – and only then move into the sound of the vowel, followed by the closing consonant/s.) The consonant /h/ can perhaps be regarded as a special kind of 'unvoiced consonant', even an 'aspirated vowel', being produced by a voiceless expulsion of air from the lungs, with no interception by lips or teeth, and the tongue in position in the mouth ready for the following vowel.

definite article designates a particular entity (represented by a noun) and assumes that the specific entity can be clearly identified by the hearer (e.g. *the Government, the library, in the front garden of that house*) (contrast the indefinite article, where no such assumption is made, e.g. *in a front garden*)

demonstrative adjectives and **demonstrative pronouns** express a contrast between near and distant entities; **demonstrative adjectives** precede a noun (e.g. *these apples; those pears*; *these ideas* v. *those ideas*); **demonstrative pronouns** stand alone (e.g. *I'll take these and then those*)

determiners appear before a noun, and any preceding adjective (e.g. *a happy event, the weekend, that day, those beautiful flowers*); see too **definite article** and **demonstrative adjectives**

glottal stop where the vocal tract is closed, causing a compression of air, which is then released in the form of a small explosion; can be heard in, say, a Cockney pronunciation of the middle 't' in words like 'bu'er' and 'compu'er' for 'butter' and 'computer'.

hypercorrection where a pronunciation feature which is perceived to be socially prestigious (e.g. /h/) is used but misjudged, for example the sounding of /h/ in *honour*, or perhaps Morel's stressed *ham* in his exclamation to the visiting minister: Tired – I ***ham*** that…*You* don't know what it is to be tired, as *I'm* tired., ***SL***, Chapter II, 46: 32-3)

intensifiers increase the quality expressed by **adjectives** or **adverbs** (e.g. *extremely beautiful*, *really carefully*)

irregular verbs see **verbs**

main verbs also known as 'full' verbs, which can stand alone and have a clearly stateable meaning, e.g. *dance, think, write, talk*; see too **verbs**

negative denial or contradiction of the truth of an assertion, statement etc.; usually expressed via such forms as *not, nothing, none, never* etc.

non-count nouns nouns (also known as mass nouns) which do not normally have a plural form (e.g *music, furniture, warmth*)

nouns express some entity, thing, creature or concept (*a table, the girl, tigers, music, truth*)

object term used for the entity which is directly affected by the process expressed by the **verb** (e.g. *he dropped a brick, the child painted my face*); some **personal pronouns** have a different form when acting as object (e.g. *He admires her, they saw me, fog surrounded us*, but this does not apply to the pronoun *you*, which has the same form whether acting as subject or object: *you found them* and *we found you*)

past tense see **verbs**

past participle see **verbs**

personal pronouns words which stand in for people or things; pronouns may be first person (*I, we*), second person (*you*) or third person (*he, she, it, they*), and may be singular or plural; subject forms are *I, you, he, she, it, we, you, they* and corresponding object forms are *me, you, him, her, it, us, you, them*; see too **possessive pronouns** and **reflexive pronouns**

plural see **singular v. plural**

possessive pronouns indicate ownership by individual/s, whether acting as determiners or standing alone: *my/mine, your/yours, his, her/hers, our/ours, your/yours, their/theirs* (e.g. *her house, their coats*, and also *that house is hers, those coats are theirs*)

prepositions express how entities mentioned in a sentence relate to each other, often in space or time; e.g. *of, in, on, to, with* etc (*end of the week, house in the wood, food on the table, I went to the cinema, at the cinema I saw 'The Boy with Green Hair'*)

present tense see **tense** and **verbs**

pronouns words which stand in place of nouns and have a range of functions: see **personal pronouns, possessive pronouns, reflexive pronouns, relative pronouns**

reflexive pronouns words which 'reflect' the individual/s already mentioned, i.e. *myself, yourself, himself, herself, itself, ourselves, yourselves, themselves* (e.g. *he warmed himself by the fire*)

regular verbs see **verbs**

relative pronoun stands in for a preceding noun or noun phrase and enables additional information to be given about the entity expressed by that noun (e.g. *the man who gave the talk*…helps us identify the man being referred to; *I saw a film that I really enjoyed* introduces the provision of more information about a particular film)

singular v. plural a contrast between 'one' and 'more than one'; a plural noun is most often indicated by the addition of the **suffix** *–s* or *–es*; the choice of a singular or plural noun or pronoun can influence the form of its related **verb**, especially a third person singular subject in the present tense (e.g. *money talks, clocks tick; the time is…, the days are; he was…, they were…*)

subject the name given to the entity which influences the form of its related **verb**

suffixes a wide range of particles attached (or 'fixed') to the end of a word; e.g. to verbs: *-s, -ing, -ed* etc. (*she talks, is talking, talked*); to nouns: *-s, -es* etc. (*a pear, two pears; a class, two classes*); to adjectives to form adverbs: *-ly* (e.g. *softly, helpfully*); (contrast prefix, which is attached to the beginning of a word, e.g. *disobey, uncomfortable, reawaken*)

tense term used for formal indication of time of action or process, mainly 'present tense' or 'past tense' of **verbs**

unvoiced consonants see **consonants v. vowels**

verbs express some action or process or state of being to which time can be attached, the main ways of expressing time being via forms of verbs which indicate present tense, past tense and the present perfect form of the past tense; the forms of **regular verbs** are *I walk, I walked, I have walked*, respectively, with **past tense** and **past participle** both being formed by the addition of **suffix** *–ed* to the **present tense** form; **irregular verbs** have three distinct forms, e.g. *I sing, I sang, I have sung*; *I take, I took, I have taken*; verbs frequently show **agreement** with their **subject** in the present tense, especially in the third person singular, when **suffix** *–s* is added to indicate agreement with a singular subject (e.g. *she walks regularly; they ramble most days; he sings in the choir; horses gallop*); the verbs *to be* and *to have* are special types of irregular verb (having the forms *I am, I was, I have been*; *I have, I had, I have had*): they can act as **main verbs** (e.g. *she is happy, I have a cold*) or as **auxiliary verbs** (e.g. *she is laughing, I have had a cold*);

voiced consonants see **consonants v. vowels**

vowels see **consonants v. vowels**

Appendix 2: Glossary of words and phrases in illustrative examples

'ae'-porth a half-penny worth – a little thing
banns proclamation in church of intended marriage
blacklegs strike-breakers
bodge up mess up
butty/ies miner/s in charge of team working a stall
cadin' tame, affectionate
cat-lick quick wash
childer children
choppers teeth (dentures in this instance)
clat-farted gossiped
claver mouth, chatter
club money payment during unemployment or sickness
consumption wasting disease (e.g. tuberculosis)
draughtin' causing a draught, a (cold) current of air
duck, ducky/ey dear, darling; **duck** (though not *ducky* or *duckey*) is also used to indicate a zero score in cricket
em'py empty (clearly a misplaced apostrophe)
fair really, quite (with verbs, adjectives); real, complete (with nouns)
gaffer boss
grounded me restricted my movements, kept me indoors (a form of punishment)
gumption common sense, shrewdness
hoom, whoam home
hoss horse
jack up ruin, damage, break up
knocked off finished work
Ladbrokes a well known firm of bookmakers, for the placing of bets on horses etc.
makin's makings, ingredients
mormin' wandering aimlessly
mun must
mealy-mouthed sanctimonious, hypocritical
mulligrubs stomach ache, bout of the miseries
nowt nothing

ormin' silly, awkward
ower over
owt anything
panchion large, shallow, earthenware bowl
paper rounds delivers newspapers on a 'round', a particular group of houses, streets etc. (used here – creatively – as a verb)
roads underground roadways and passages in pit
scraight scream, weep, cry
scullery room off kitchen for washing, laundry etc.
slives, slivin' sneaks, creeps, sneaking, creeping
sluther slide, shuffle
smockravelled mixed up, puzzled, confused
spotted dick a particularly rich suet pudding containing currants, sultanas etc., served as dessert
stall, sta' section of coal face allocated to team of miners
stint day's work, set task
summat something
telly informal term for television set
'ussy hussy, slovenly or immoral woman
waftin' waving, flapping
whoam, hoom home

Appendix 3: Annotated bibliography

Crystal, David, *Rediscover Grammar*. Harlow, Essex: Pearson Longman, 3rd edition 2004. [An accessible and often entertaining description of the grammar of English; essentially a kind of potted version of the Quirk et al grammar, *op.cit*, to which it is explicitly related.]

Edwards, V. K., P. Trudgill and B. Weltens, *The Grammar of English Dialect: A Survey of Research*. London: Economic and Social Science Research Council, 1984. [Contains a detailed listing of non-standard grammatical forms occurring in British dialects of English as found in research studies up to 1982. A number of these forms are identifiable in the Erewash Valley dialect.]

Hillier, Hilary, *The Language of Spontaneous Interaction between Children aged 7-12: Instigating Action – Monographs in Systemic Linguistics No. 4*. Department of English Studies, University of Nottingham, 1992. [Published version of 1990 Ph.D thesis, which investigated degrees of success achieved by different utterances in bringing about specific actions during the playing of the computer game Adventureland by three children, two boys aged 12 and 7 and a girl aged 11; it related specific utterances to the particular grammatical forms chosen by the children in each case.]

Hillier, Hilary, *Analysing Real Texts: Research Studies in Modern English Language*. Basingstoke: Palgrave Macmillan, 2004. [Intended mainly for university or college students. Chapter 7, 'Fictional Narrative in a Regional Dialect', analyses a passage from a novella called *Our Mam un t'Others*, written and then read aloud by Fred Wetherill, a retired miner. It is a first-person narrative in the persona of a young member of a mining family using the dialect of Kirkby-in-Ashfield, Nottinghamshire, a small town within the

Erewash Valley. Chapter 5, 'Children's Talk', analyses extracts from the speech of two junior school children in Eastwood on 30 June 1992 (see some extracts quoted in Chapter 4), but, instead of examining dialect choices, it assesses the children's differing linguistic strategies according to whether they are just conversing ('Talk' data) or actually engaged in playing a computer game ('Task' data).]

Hillier, Hilary, Matches and mismatches: patterns of THOU and YOU in *The Merry-go-Round. Journal of the D H Lawrence Society*, 2004-5, pp. 83-102. [Takes different characters' use of the pronouns *thou* and *you* as the basis for exploring complex romantic entanglements within a mining community.]

Hillier, Hilary, Community, family, 'Morel': a dialect approach to *Sons and Lovers*. To appear in the proceedings of the 11th D H Lawrence International Conference, 2007: *Return to Eastwood*. Nottingham: New Ventures/CCC Press, forthcoming. [Relates dialect use by individual members of the Morel family to the language of the surrounding community, and considers the implications of similarity and difference. It incorporates an earlier version of the framework set out in this book. It also includes sections which compare uses of *tha* by both Paul Morel and his brother Arthur and their possible meanings in particular circumstances.]

Hughes, Arthur, Peter Trudgill and Dominic Watt, *English Accents and Dialects: An Introduction to Social and Regional Varieties of English in the British Isles*. London: Hodder Arnold, 4th edition, 2005. [An invaluable introduction to British dialects. It surveys and describes the variety of grammatical and phonological features to be found across the British Isles, a number of which are identifiable in the

Erewash Valley dialect. It includes a CD consisting of edited interviews with speakers from different areas.]

Milroy, James and Lesley Milroy, eds, *Real English: The Grammar of English Dialects in the British Isles*. London: Longman, 1993. [A collection of papers on different aspects of dialect grammar, including historical and social factors in grammatical variation and case studies showing the kinds of grammatical forms found in selected regions of Britain and Ireland. It includes an extensive Directory of English Dialect Resources.]

Montes Granado, Consuelo, *D. H. Lawrence: El Dialecto en sus Novelas.* Acta Salmanticensia, Estudios Filologicos 234, University of Salamanca, 1990. [An impressively-detailed survey in Spanish of the phonology, morphology, syntax and lexis of the Erewash Valley dialect as represented in a wide range of Lawrence's stories, novels and plays. A valuable resource in providing some supplementary textual data and, coincidentally, confirming aspects of the general approach adopted by this book.]

Odour of Chrysanthemums: A Text in Process, The University of Nottingham (**http://longford.nottingham.ac.uk/ooc/**). [A project in which four different versions of 'Odour of Chrysanthemums' are presented, three of which have been converted to electronic text format. Detailed comparative analyses of the three electronic texts are displayed. The site includes supporting materials of various kinds, including an earlier version of the framework set out in this book, illustrated by extracts taken from all three analysed versions of the story.]

Quirk, Randolph, Sidney Greenbaum, Geoffrey Leech and Jan Svartvik, *A Comprehensive Grammar of the English*

Language. London: Longman, 1985 (revised edition 1991). [A monumental description of the grammar of English, an invaluable aid in compiling and classifying the dialect grammar of the Erewash Valley in that it complements and refines, where appropriate, some of the terms used by Edwards et al, *op.cit.* and Hughes et al, *op.cit.*]

Scollins, Richard and John Titford, *Ey Up Mi Duck!* Parts One, Two and Three. Ilkeston: Scollins & Titford, 1976, 1977. [Non-specialist books, intended for the general reader, which contain much useful information on various aspects of the dialect of Ilkeston, Derbyshire (a town in the Erewash Valley).]

Traugott, Elizabeth Closs and Mary Louise Pratt, *Linguistics for Students of Literature*. New York: Harcourt Brace Jovanovich, 1980. [The title speaks for itself. Chapter 8, on regional, social and ethnic varieties of English, contains a particularly illuminating section on 'Stereotypic versus Variable Representations of Language Varieties' and considers the significance of intended or expected readership. The term 'non-standard' or 'non-conventional' spellings is to be preferred, however, to their choice of 'deviant spellings'.]

Trudgill, Peter, *The Dialects of England*. Oxford: Blackwell, 2nd edition, 1999. [A broad survey of traditional and modern dialects of England identifying major geographical and linguistic regions and sub-regions within them.]

Acknowledgments

I would like to express my appreciation and thanks to the following: the children and teachers of Devonshire Drive Infants and Junior Schools and Greasley Beauvale Infants School, and to various residents of Eastwood and surrounding area who have helped to provide me with linguistic data; to Nottinghamshire County Council for supporting the initial stages of the project, and to Kim Disney for her valiant efforts in making the first drafts of transcripts of the children's talk; to Madeline Bostock for discussing the use of a number of interesting constructions with me; to Margaret Berry, Ron Carter, Carol Debney, Sean Matthews and John Worthen for their encouragement during the long gestation of the framework and eventual book, and for their many helpful suggestions and comments on early versions (its inevitable shortcomings remain, of course, my entire responsibility); finally, and as always, to Edd and Dan for their patience with me and their cheerful provision of reassurance and technical support!

The author and publisher are grateful to Pollinger Limited and the Estate of Frieda Lawrence Ravagli for permission to quote from Lawrence's works.

www.ingramcontent.com/pod-product-compliance
Ingram Content Group UK Ltd.
Pitfield, Milton Keynes, MK11 3LW, UK
UKHW042002190726
13854UKWH00005B/2127

9 781905 510184